DISASTER ALERT!

SPACE DISASTER AND METEORITE ALERT!

Julie Karner

Crabtree Publishing Company
www.crabtreebooks.com

DISASTER ALERT!

presented by:

Crabtree Publishing Company

www.crabtreebooks.com

Coordinating editor: Ellen Rodger

Project editor: Adrianna Morganelli

Editors: Rachel Eagen, Carrie Gleason

Book design and production coordinator: Rosie Gowsell

Production assistant: Samara Parent

Scanning technician: Arlene Arch-Wilson

Art Director: Rob MacGregor

Photo research: Allison Napier

Consultant: Dr. Richard Cheel, Earth Sciences Department, Brock University

Photographs: AP/ AP Wide World Photos: p. 12 (bottom), p. 13, p. 17 (both), p. 27 (both); Bettmann/ Corbis: p. 15 (bottom), p. 16, p. 25 (bottom); Jonathan Blair/ Corbis: p. 7 (bottom) Digital image © 1996 Corbis; Original image courtesy of NASA/ Corbis: p. 9 (bottom), p. 18; NASA/ Roger Ressmeyer/ Corbis: p. 12 (top); Roger Ressmeyer/ Corbis: p. 22; Reuters/ Corbis: p. 20, p. 23 (both); Denis Scott/ Corbis: p. 28; Stapleton Collection/ Corbis: p. 29 (top); Fotosearch: cover; Michael Gaylard PhD: p. 14; NASA/ SSPL/ The Image Works: p. 1; Julian Baum/ Photo Researchers, Inc.: p. 26; Calif. Assoc. for Research in Astronomy/ Photo Researchers, Inc.: p. 7 (top); Lynette Cook/ Photo Researchers, Inc.: p. 29 (bottom); Mark Garlick/ Photo Researchers, Inc.: pp. 6-7; NASA/ Photo Researchers, Inc.: p. 24; Novosti/ Photo Researchers, Inc.: p. 25 (top); David Parker/ Photo Researchers, Inc.: p. 4; Science Source/ Photo Researchers Inc.: p. 5; Gianni Tortoli/ Photo Researchers, Inc.: p. 19 (bottom); NASA/ Science Photo Library: p. 15 (top). Other images from stock photo cd.

Illustrations: Dan Pressman: pp. 10-11; David Wysotski: pp. 30-31

Cover: A meteorite is a piece of space debris that passes through the atmosphere and hits the Earth, creating a depression, or crater.

Contents: The surface of the Moon is covered with craters produced by meteor impacts.

Title page: During the early years of spaceflight, the American and Russian space programs experienced many failures, such as rockets exploding upon liftoff.

Crabtree Publishing Company

www.crabtreebooks.com 1-800-387-7650

Cataloging-in-Publication Data

Karner, Julie, 1976-

Space disaster and meteorite alert! / written by Julie Karner.

p. cm. -- (Disaster alert!)

Includes index.

ISBN-13: 978-0-7787-1583-2 (RLB)

ISBN-10: 0-7787-1583-3 (RLB)

ISBN-13: 978-0-7787-1615-0 (pbk.)

ISBN-10: 0-7787-1615-5 (pbk.)

1. Astronautics--Accidents--Juvenile literature. 2. Meteorite craters--Juvenile literature. I. Title. II. Series.

TL867.K37 2005

363.12'4--dc22 2005014744

LC

Published in the United States
PMB 16A
350 Fifth Ave.
Suite 3308
New York, NY
10118

Published in Canada
616 Welland Ave.
St. Catharines
Ontario, Canada
L2M 5V6

Published in the United Kingdom
73 Lime Walk
Headington
Oxford
OX3 7AD
United Kingdom

Published in Australia
386 Mt. Alexander Rd.
Ascot Vale (Melbourne)
VIC 3032

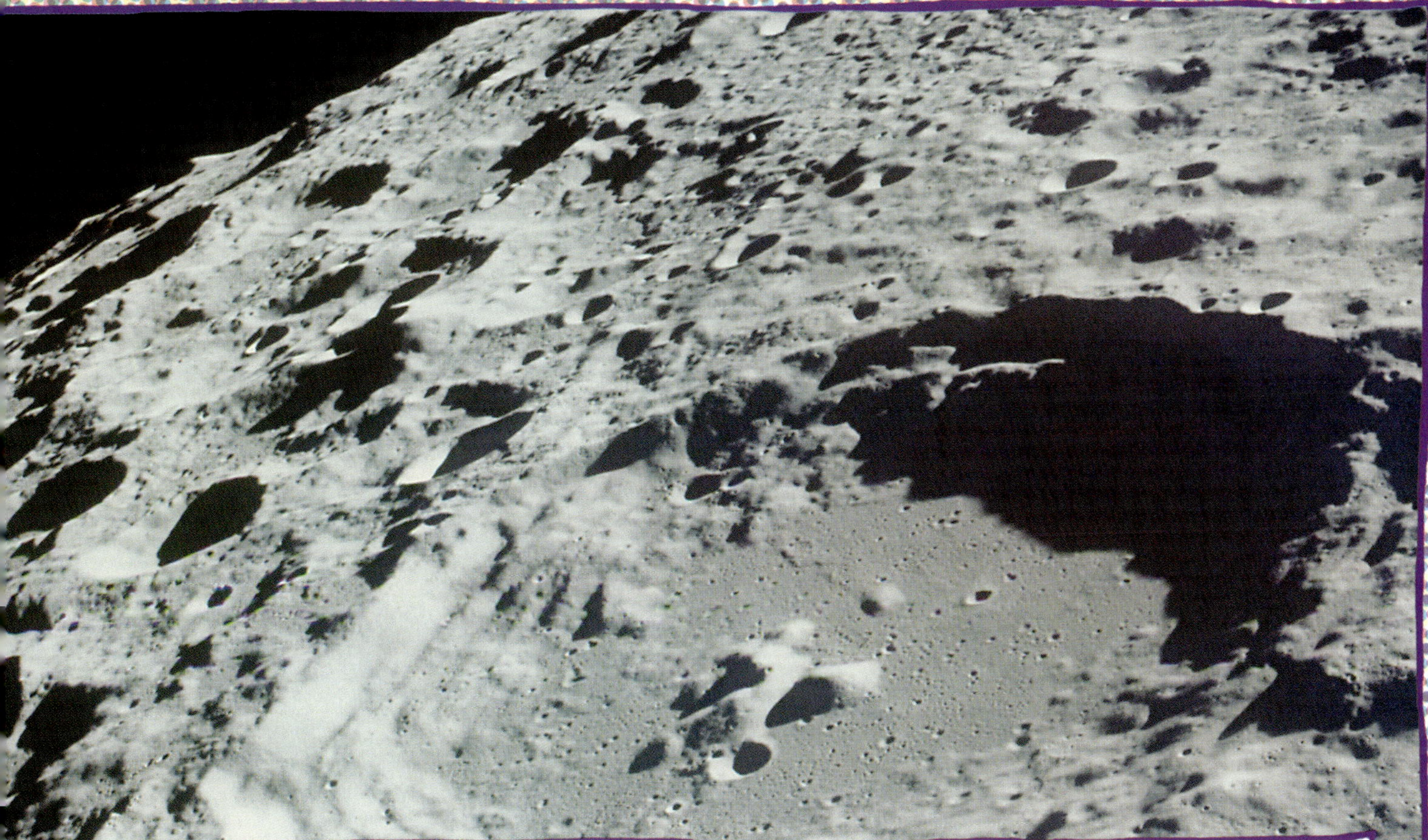

Table of Contents

Infinite Dangers

Arizona, U.S.A.

For centuries, the sight of shooting stars and comets has created wonder for some people and fear for others. For those with an adventurous spirit, the vast reaches of space invite exploration. With the beauty and mystery of space comes the possibility of danger and the threat of disaster.

People's fear of death from the sky is not completely unreasonable. The collision of a comet or large asteroid with Earth could be disastrous. A relatively small meteorite explosion over a large city could cause hundreds of thousands of deaths. Many scientists believe that 65 million years ago, the collision of an asteroid or comet approximately six miles (ten kilometers) wide with Earth caused the **extinction** of the dinosaurs. The impact of a large meteorite colliding with Earth could end life on the planet.

What is a disaster? A disaster is a destructive event that affects the natural world and human communities. Some disasters are predictable and others occur without warning. Coping successfully with a disaster often depends on a community's preparation.

(above) Meteor Crater, also called the Barringer Crater, in Arizona, in the United States, was formed by a meteorite that hit Earth. It is about 50,000 years old, and about 656 feet (200 meters) deep and 3,937 feet (1200 meters) across.

Human contribution

When people began to explore the universe, space disasters of another kind began to occur. In the 1960s, the United States and the Soviet Union embarked on a race to put the first person in orbit around Earth, and then to land the first person on the Moon. Early attempts at space exploration produced accidents that claimed the lives of many people. In the years to follow, many advances were made in the study and exploration of space, but accidents have continued to claim the lives of astronauts.

(below) When Halley's Comet returned in 1986, astronomers observed it from the ground and from space. It is predicted that the comet will next return in 2061.

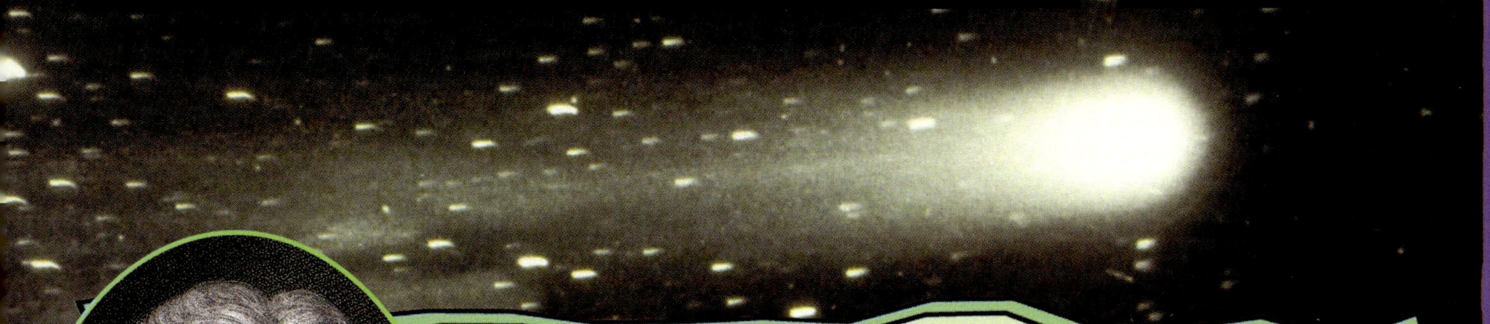

Halley's Comet Myths

Ancient peoples believed that comets were signs of war, **famine**, or death to come. The appearance of a comet, later known as Halley's Comet, in 1066, inspired mass terror in Europe and was blamed for the death of England's King Harold II in the Battle of Hastings. In 1665, Europeans believed that the deaths of thousands of people from the **bubonic plague**, or the Black Death, were caused by the passage of Halley's Comet. In 1910, Earth was scheduled to pass through the tail of Halley's Comet. Scientists reported that poisonous gases in the comet's tail would kill Earth's population. People tried to profit from the scare by selling "comet pills," which they promised would protect humans from the poisonous gases. Some people committed suicide rather than face the effects of the comet. Despite the panic, Halley's Comet passed without causing any harm to life on Earth.

(above) In 1682, English astronomer Edmond Halley determined that the comet took 76 years to orbit the Sun. The comet was named for Halley when, in 1758, it returned as he had predicted.

Natural Disasters

The solar system **is made up of celestial bodies that travel in orbits, or set paths, around the Sun. The largest are the nine planets, and others range from rocks miles (kilometers) in diameter to dust particles smaller than a grain of sand. Earth is threatened with disaster when medium to large-sized celestial bodies stray from their orbits and approach Earth's** atmosphere**.**

Asteroids

The two major types of bodies in solar orbit are comets and asteroids. Asteroids are made up of rock or metal, usually nickel or iron, or a mixture of both. Most asteroids are located in the asteroid belt, an area between Mars and Jupiter that contains thousands of small rocky fragments. While most asteroids are less than 62 miles (100 kilometers) in diameter, astronomers have documented about 200 asteroids that each span hundreds of miles (kilometers).

Objects in orbit

The term meteoroid is used for space debris that orbits the Sun, such as rocks knocked loose from Mars or the Moon, or pieces of rock or metal that have strayed from a comet's orbit. A meteor is a small piece of rock, metal, or dust that enters Earth's atmosphere. Traveling very fast, the meteor pushes the air in front of it. The pressure built up from the **friction** of the meteor and the gas **molecules** in the atmosphere causes it to heat up and glow. The glowing meteors, or shooting stars, burn up before they hit the ground. A meteorite is a piece of space debris that passes through the atmosphere and reaches Earth's surface. A meteorite's speed is so great that it creates a depression, or crater, upon impact.

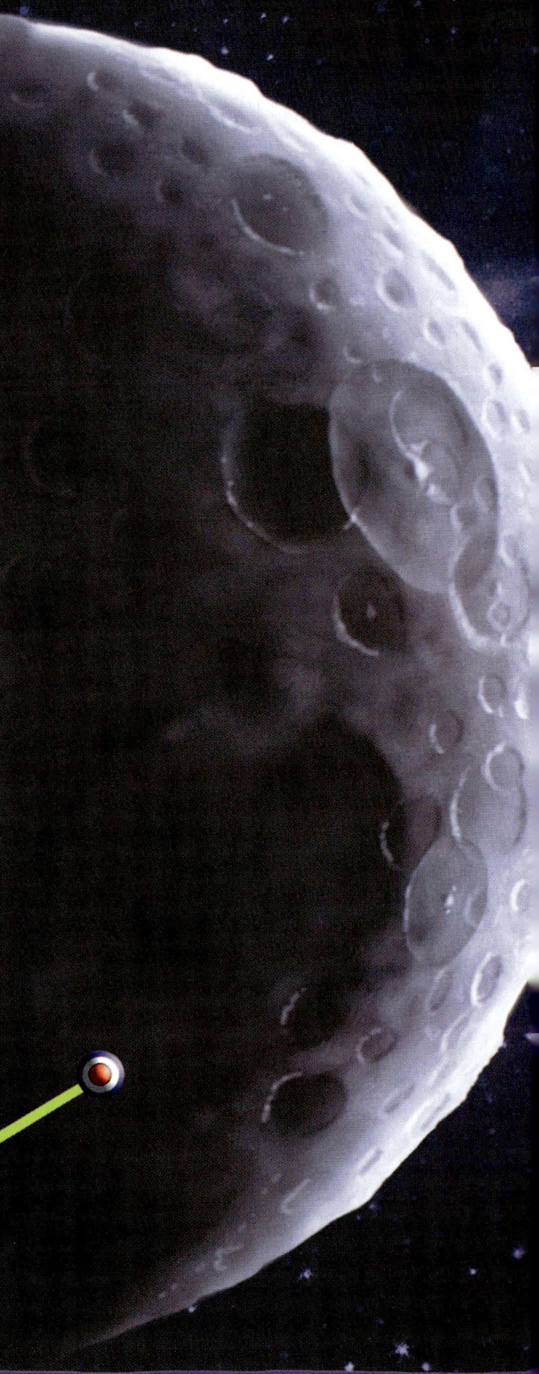

Millions of asteroids are found in the asteroid belt. The largest known asteroid, Ceres, is 589 miles (948 kilometers) in diameter.

Comets

Most comets are located in the Oort Cloud, a spherical area that surrounds the solar system. Others come from the Kuiper Belt, a disc that extends from Neptune's orbital path. Comets have a dense core, or nucleus, of rock or metal, coated by an icy layer of frozen water and gases that contains rock fragments and particles of dust. As a comet approaches the Sun along its orbital path, the ice melts into a gaseous cloud. The **solar winds** blow the dust and gases into two separate tails.

When comets crash

When a comet passes near the Sun, the force of the solar winds separate some of the dust and gases from the main body of the comet. The ever-changing shape and composition of the comet can also change its path. As the comet decreases in mass, it can become less resistant to the pull of **gravity** from the planets it passes, and be pulled off course. A comet that strikes the Earth would have catastrophic effects on nature and civilization.

(above) While passing Jupiter in 1992, comet Shoemaker-Levy 9 became trapped by the planet's gravity and broke up into pieces. In 1994, the fragments crashed onto Jupiter's surface. Two small light areas near the bottom of the picture reveal where Jupiter was hit.

(left) School children visit the American Museum of Natural History and touch the Ahnighito Meteorite, the world's second largest meteorite.

Exploration Disasters

Space exploration is an exciting challenge, but with it comes many dangers. Beyond initial blast-off, a mission faces challenges from orbiting around the Earth and withstanding the harsh environment of space, to a safe return home.

Getting off the ground

A spacecraft needs a lot of fuel to achieve speeds fast enough to travel beyond Earth's atmosphere. It must push off from the Earth's surface with enough force to resist the pull of gravity. The fuel is mixed with liquid **oxygen** to create a controlled explosion to propel the craft upward. Care is taken to ensure that these **flammable** and explosive materials are sealed and stored away from sources of spark or fire. A miscalculation in the rate at which the oxygen and fuel are mixed could cause an explosion and destroy the craft.

Dangers in space

Earth's atmosphere protects the planet from small meteoroids, dangerous gases, and extreme temperatures. Beyond the atmosphere, a spacecraft is exposed to the extreme heat of the Sun's rays, which reach temperatures of 392°F to 842°F (200°C to 450°C). On the side of the craft facing away from the Sun, the temperature drops to a cool -256°F to -454°F (-160°C to -270°C). Spacecrafts must be well insulated for both temperature extremes so their components do not melt or freeze.

(left) A speed of 17,000 mph (27,350 km/h) is necessary for a spacecraft to maintain Earth orbit. If the craft speeds up, it will veer off into space. If it slows down, it will crash into Earth's atmosphere, where it will burn up or hit the Earth's surface.

Dangers for astronauts

Gravity is severely reduced in space, which causes changes in an astronaut's body. The heart can become weak because it is no longer pumping blood against the force of gravity, and internal organs may change shape or position. Astronauts are actually almost three inches (eight centimeters) taller in space without Earth's gravity pulling downward on their spines. A special exercise program is required to keep astronauts healthy and counteract the effects of weightlessness. **Nutrient** requirements are very strict in space because illness could bring an early end to a mission. Specially prepared foods containing a proper balance of vitamins, minerals, and healthy ingredients are essential to keep astronauts functioning at their full potential.

(above) Astronauts' spacesuits are designed to provide breathable oxygen, guard against temperature extremes, toxic gases, radiation, and micrometeorites, which are tiny particles of space debris that can tear holes in even tough materials due to their rapid speed.

A small pit in the glass window of this space shuttle was caused by space debris or a meteoroid. While in Earth's orbit, space shuttles are exposed to small asteroids and pieces of rock or metal from Mars, the Moon, or a comet's orbit, that can damage the shuttle upon impact.

Life of an Asteroid

More than 3,400 documented asteroids belong to a group known as Near Earth Objects, or NEOs. These asteroids travel in orbits that approach or cross Earth's orbital path, threatening a collision with Earth.

Changes in orbit

An asteroid's orbit can change if it collides with other asteroids, planets, or space debris. Orbits can also be changed if an asteroid passes close enough to one of the planets to be affected by its gravitational pull. As a result, an asteroid that normally passes at a safe distance of a million miles (1,609,300 km) from Earth could suddenly impact the planet.

Crash!: An Asteroid's Journey

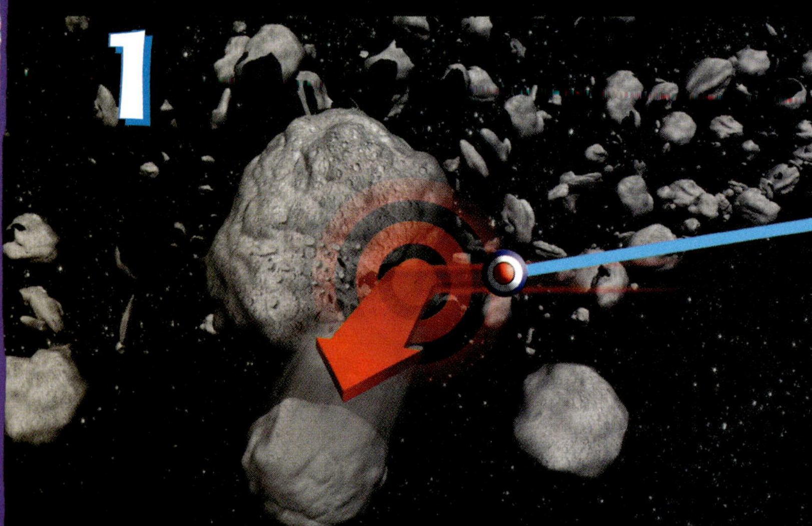

1. A large asteroid within the asteroid belt collides with another, causing it to be bumped off of its original orbital path.

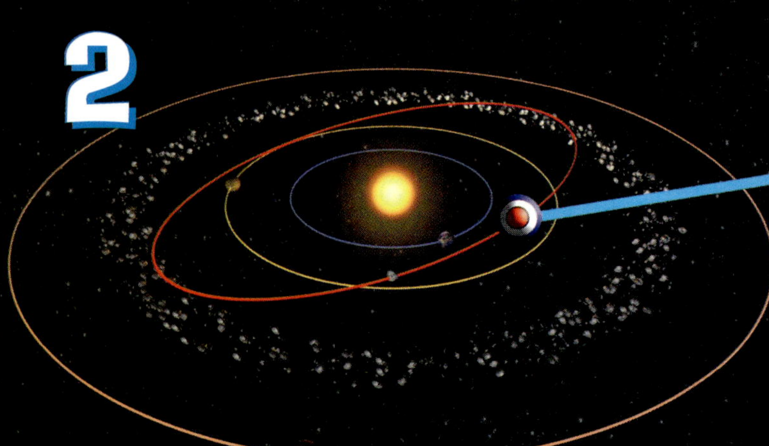

2. The asteroid follows a new orbit around the Sun, which brings it close to the Earth's orbital path, making it a Near Earth Object. The asteroid is also close to the orbital path of other planets, such as Jupiter, or a comet that also orbits the Sun. At this stage, it is called a meteoroid.

3. The gravitational forces around a planet, such as Jupiter, pull on the meteoroid as it passes, causing a slight shift in its orbital path. The orbital paths of the Earth and the meteoroid meet, which sends the meteoroid hurtling toward Earth.

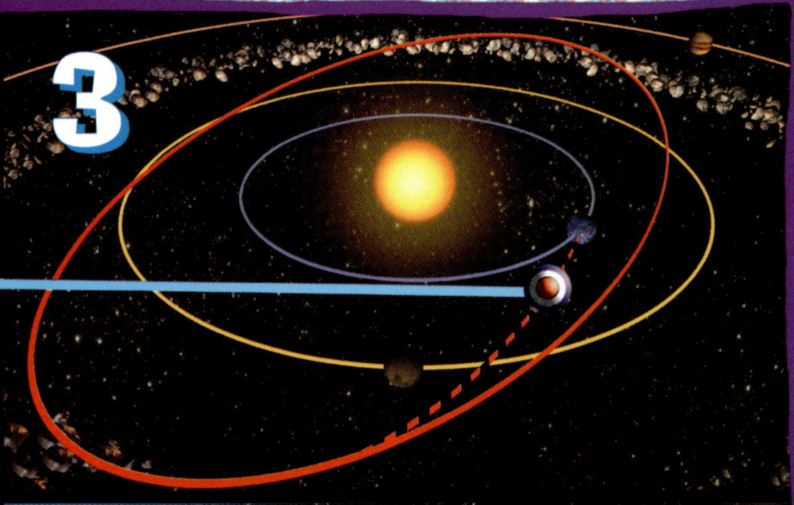

4. The meteoroid hurtles through space at great speed and enters Earth's atmosphere. The force of its combined mass and speed produces a huge buildup of energy in the form of friction as it pushes through the atmosphere.

5. The meteoroid ends its journey in a fiery and energetic collision with the Earth's surface. At this stage, the meteoroid becomes a meteorite because it has landed on Earth.

6. The force of the collision causes an explosion, and the impact blasts a crater in the Earth's surface far wider and deeper than the meteorite itself.

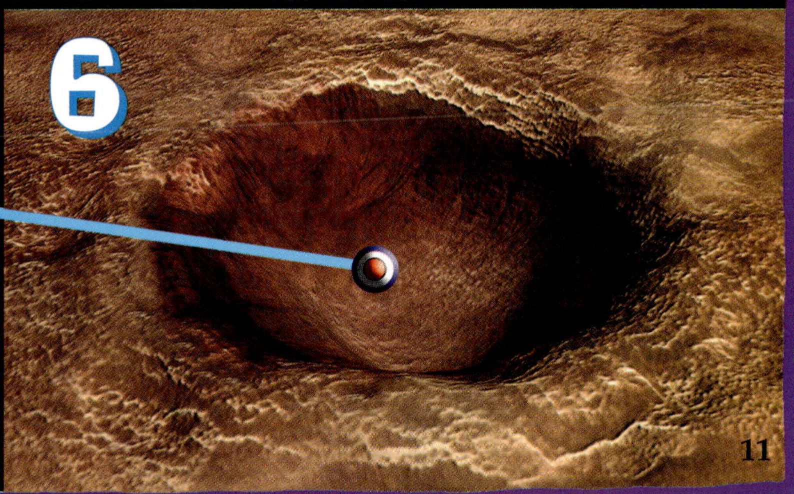

Failed Space Mission

One of the most expensive space exploration disasters in recent history is that of the Mars Climate Orbiter and Mars Polar Lander, crafts that were launched to learn more about the planet Mars.

The goal of the mission

The Mars Climate Orbiter was designed in the 1990s to study the planet's weather for the 687-day period it takes for Mars to orbit the Sun. By gathering information about pressure, dust, temperature, and water vapor in Mars' atmosphere, astronomers, **geologists,** and climatologists hoped to learn how the planet's climate has changed over time, and better understand climate change on Earth. The device was to relay data to and from the Mars Polar Lander, which was to search for evidence of water or ice in the soil near the southern pole of Mars. Evidence of a water source on Mars could support the theory that **microscopic** life forms once existed on Mars.

(right) A Delta II rocket lifts off with NASA's Mars Climate Orbiter from the Cape Canaveral Air Station in Florida. The Orbiter was launched to provide scientists with clues to the planet's early climate history and information about possible water reserves ***beneath the surface. Scientists believe the Orbiter's satellite burned up in Mars' atmosphere, or veered off into space on a path orbiting the Sun.***

Reaching Mars

On December 11, 1998, the Mars Climate Orbiter was launched aboard a Delta II rocket from Florida, in the United States. The rocket sent the Orbiter beyond Earth's atmosphere before it was released. Scientists from the National Aeronautics and Space Administration, or NASA, adjusted the Orbiter's trajectory, or path, to set it on course for Mars. After traveling almost ten months and 416 million miles (670 million kilometers), it arrived on schedule on September 23, 1999. As the Orbiter prepared to enter Mars' atmosphere, it passed out of view behind the planet. The scientists monitoring the mission's progress never saw the Orbiter again.

What happened?

Studies of the mission revealed that human error caused the mission's failure. Two teams from NASA worked on the Mars Climate Orbiter. One team worked on its design and technical operations. The other team designed the computer programs used to plan its course. While building the Orbiter and preparing it for launch, one team used metric units for measurements and calculations, while the other used imperial units. The difference between centimeters and inches proved catastrophic for the mission. When the Orbiter attempted to enter Mars' orbit, it was 106 miles (170 kilometers) closer to the planet's surface than it should have been.

(below) A NASA employee demonstrates the robotic arm operation on a life-sized model of the 2001 Mars Orbiter. The robotic arm is similar to the one on the Mars Polar Lander.

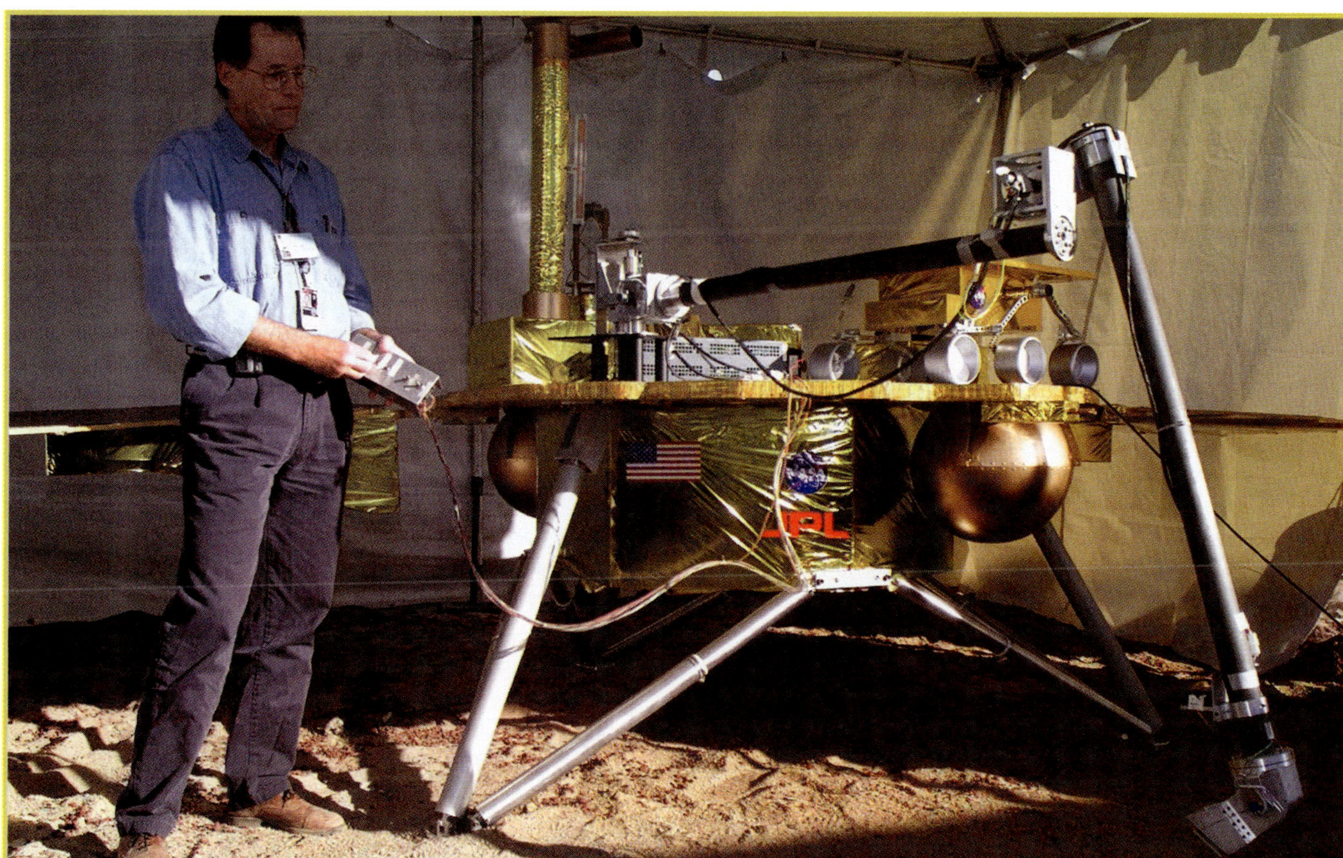

Famous Impacts

Meteorites 0.04 inches (about one millimeter) in diameter strike Earth's surface about once every 30 seconds, and many more are deflected **or burned up in the atmosphere. More than 170 impact craters have been found on Earth.**

Oceanic crater

While about 70 percent of the Earth's surface is covered by water, only one oceanic meteorite strike has been documented. Scientists believe the asteroid Eltanin struck the Bellingshausen Sea off the coast of Antarctica 2.15 million years ago. Eltanin's size is estimated at 0.6 to 2.5 miles (1 to 4 km) in diameter. The impact generated a column of water 3 miles (5 km) high, causing waves as high as 130 feet (40 meters). The waves devastated the coasts of Antarctica and South America, and dust and **sediment** were propelled 2,500 miles (4,000 km) from the impact site.

Mexico

A crater ranging from 112 to 186 miles (180 to 300 km) wide was discovered on the Yucatan Peninsula in Mexico by a team of geologists searching for oil in the 1980s. The impact site is famous due to a theory proposed by scientists Luis and Walter Alvarez, that an asteroid or comet about 6 miles (10 km) in diameter was responsible for the extinction of the dinosaurs at the end of the **Cretaceous Period**. The dinosaur extinction and the formation of the Yucatan crater both occurred 65 million years ago, which supports the theory.

(above) The Tswaing crater impact site, 24.9 miles (40 km) north of Pretoria in South Africa attracts 12,000 tourists each year. The 220,000 year-old crater is about 0.62 miles (one kilometer) wide, and is one of the best-preserved meteorite craters.

The Vredefort impact crater in South Africa is over 155 miles (250 kilometers) wide. It is the oldest known impact crater on the planet, estimated to be over two billion years old.

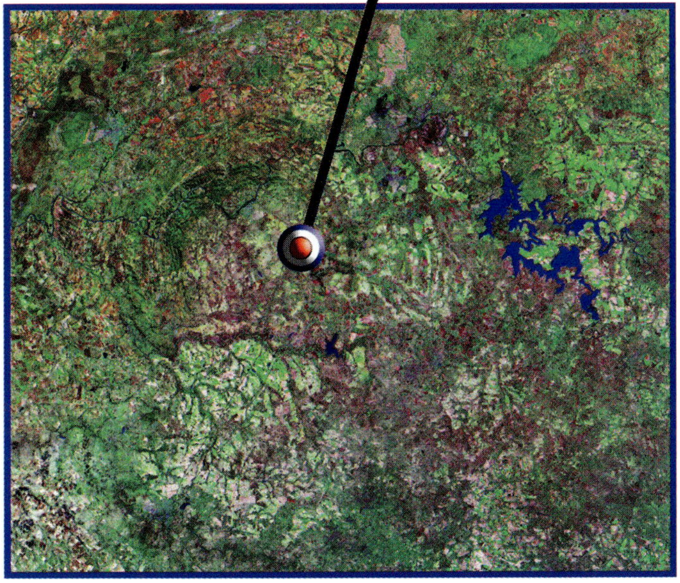

Siberia

On June 30, 1908, a massive explosion took place near the village of Tunguska in Russian Siberia. Witnesses described a giant fireball falling towards Earth hundreds of miles (kilometers) away. Trees were laid flat in a circular area that extended 15 miles (25 kilometers) in all directions from the center of the blast. Evidence of an impact crater could not be found, and studies of the Tunguska site are still ongoing. Based on chemicals found in soil samples from the impact site, some scientists believe that a comet exploded over the area. Others used computer modelling to conclude that a stony asteroid about 200 feet (60 meters) in diameter was responsible for the destruction.

Crash!

On November 30, 1954, Elizabeth Ann Hodges escaped with a severe bruise when she was struck by a meteorite that crashed through the roof of her home in Alabama, in the United States. The meteorite struck a wooden radio cabinet in her living room, bounced off, and landed on her hip. The 8.5 pound (3.86 kilogram) meteorite was donated to the University of Alabama's Museum of Natural History in 1956, where it can still be seen today.

Famous Disasters

The most tragic space disasters are those that result in loss of life. Of more than 100 space-related deaths, many occurred on takeoff or atmosphere reentry, but the majority have taken place on the ground.

In 1970, the three astronauts aboard the Apollo 13 spacecraft were faced with grave danger when a leak was discovered in the craft's oxygen tank. Working on advice from the ground crew, the astronauts managed to safely return to Earth, and were rescued after splashing down into the Pacific Ocean.

Apollo 1

In 1967, the American Apollo space program planned the Apollo 1 mission, which was to launch a manned spacecraft into orbit to prepare for the future moon landing of Apollo 11. During a training exercise on the launch pad, a spark ignited the flammable interior of the craft, and a fire spread quickly throughout the compartment. Three astronauts were unable to open the escape hatch, and were trapped inside and died. After the tragic accident, the Apollo 2 and 3 missions were cancelled.

Soyuz 1

In the 1960s, the Soviet Union was in a race against the United States to put the first man on the Moon. Vladimir Komarov was the lone **cosmonaut** aboard the Russian spacecraft Soyuz 1 in 1967. During the launch, a solar panel designed to collect the Sun's energy to help power the spacecraft's maneuvers became damaged. A repair mission by the Soyuz 2 was scheduled for liftoff the next day. Rain storms prevented the Soyuz 2 launch, and it was decided that the Soyuz 1 would make an early return to the Soviet Union. The craft's parachute failed to open on reentry into Earth's atmosphere, and the Soyuz 1 crashed in a field, killing Komarov.

Soyuz 11

The Soyuz 11's mission was to bring a crew of cosmonauts to the first space station in Earth orbit, Salyut 1. The Soyuz 11 was launched in 1971, but the mission ended in 24 days after a telescope malfunction and a minor fire. When the craft returned to Earth, it was discovered that the three cosmonauts had not survived the return trip. Before reentry into Earth's atmosphere, the craft's oxygen leaked out from an open valve into space. The air pressure in the cabin dropped to zero, which proved fatal for the astronauts.

Debris from the space shuttle Columbia streaks across the sky over Tyler, Texas, on February 1, 2003. The Columbia exploded, killing all seven astronauts, just 16 minutes before it was supposed to land in Florida.

Columbia

The Columbia, the world's first reusable spacecraft, first launched in 1981. Before the Columbia, a spacecraft was disposed of after only one mission. The Columbia was designed to land on an airstrip rather than parachuting into the ocean as previous crafts had. After 28 flights, the Columbia and its crew met a tragic end on February 1, 2003. Damage to tiles on the craft's wing, which were designed to protect against the extreme heat of reentry, caused the craft to explode in the atmosphere. All seven crew members were killed.

(right) The crew of the space shuttle Columbia wave to onlookers on their way to Launch Pad 39A for liftoff on January 16, 2003, at Cape Canaveral, Florida.

Studying Space

Scientists study past natural space disasters in an effort to predict and, if possible, avoid future disasters.

Quebec, Canada

(above) Many meteorite impacts remain undocumented because the craters have since been covered by vegetation, filled with water, or have eroded away over time. Lake Manicouagan in Quebec, Canada, is an impact crater that was created about two billion years ago.

Searching for clues

By examining the depth, diameter, and shape of an impact crater, scientists are able to determine the meteorite's size, speed, direction and angle from which it approached, and when it hit the Earth. Scientists study the fracture patterns, or tiny scrapes and cracks, in rocks found in craters, as well as large deposits of materials normally found in asteroids or comets.

Who studies potential disasters?

Many scientists work to predict potential space disasters to warn world space agencies and governments when Earth is threatened. Numerous projects, such as the European Spaceguard Foundation, as well as the Spaceguard Survey and the LINEAR search program in the United States, scan the solar system with high-powered telescopes and electronic cameras, watching for Near Earth Objects (NEOs). There still remains a large number of undocumented meteoroids orbiting near Earth. Scientists take comfort that a meteorite capable of causing a global catastrophe is only likely to impact Earth once or twice every million years.

The Hubble Space Telescope is a huge telescope that has been in Earth orbit since 1990. Since its launch, it has provided astronomers with incredible images of celestial bodies and events within the solar system and in distant galaxies.

Research Equipment

Astronomers use the Torino Scale to rate the likelihood of a meteoroid impacting Earth, as well as the meteoroid's energy, which is determined by its speed and mass. The scale ranges from zero to ten, with zero indicating an event with no probable consequences to Earth, and ten indicating a definite global catastrophe.

(right) In the early 1600s, Italian scientist Galileo Galilei created the first telescope able to magnify objects in space. He used this tool to gather evidence for his theory that the Earth revolved around the Sun, which was not commonly believed at the time.

Exploring Space

Space exploration missions are very large operations organized by government-run space agencies that work independently or with other nations. Many space agencies monitor space for signs of potentially dangerous objects.

Who explores space?

The largest and most famous organization dedicated to space exploration is NASA, which was established on October 1, 1958, in the United States. NASA's main headquarters are in Washington, D.C., and their launch facilities are in Florida. There are about 40 space programs around the world in countries such as China, Britain, Japan, Bangladesh, Peru, and Indonesia.

The National Aeronautics and Space Administration (NASA) is one of the world's leading forces in space exploration and scientific research.

Global-scale disasters

On November 1, 2000, a document entitled "The International Charter of Space and Major Disasters" was signed by seven international space agencies. They agreed that a system of gathering and sharing information about large-scale natural or man-made disasters would be made. To date, the agencies have dealt with natural disasters such as floods and droughts since there have not been any immediate meteorite threats. The United Nations is an organization of 191 countries whose goal is to solve international problems by global cooperation. In the event of a global meteorite threat, the United Nations would discuss options to deal with the issue and devise a plan of action.

The cost of space exploration

Space exploration is a very expensive task. Space organizations that are run by a nation's government receive their funds from taxpayers. In 1989, United States President George Bush proposed plans for an orbiting space station where spacecrafts could dock to refuel, and experiments could be carried out. The plan also included a return to the Moon to develop colonies in which humans can live, work, and perform scientific experiments. These colonies would provide an initial testing ground for the long-term goal of a manned mission to Mars. The cost of this ongoing plan is estimated at $190 billion over the next 30 years. The money will be used to build space vehicles, computer software, robotics, and other scientific developments that make space exploration possible.

Space stations are large satellites designed to support a human crew and remain in Earth orbit for long periods of time. Space journeys are launched from space stations, which serve as bases for conducting research, refueling space shuttles, and repairing satellites.

Preventing Disaster

The fear of future major meteorite impacts that result in a huge loss of life has motivated scientists to find the means to predict and prevent such a disaster.

This charge-coupled device, or CCD, is like the ones used aboard the Hubble Space Telescope. A CCD is a special camera.

When will doomsday come?

Space agencies have yet to identify a meteorite so large that its collision on Earth would forever alter life on the planet. This does not mean that no such meteorite exists. There is an estimated 2,000 Near Earth Objects in space with diameters greater than 0.62 miles (1 km), but only about 100 have had their orbits mapped out. Small, but dangerous, meteoroids with diameters of less than 0.62 miles (1 km) could avoid detection until collision is unavoidable. Collisions among asteroids within the asteroid belt can also send unmapped meteoroids hurtling toward Earth.

Predicting disaster

In order to predict a potential collision with Earth, scientists continuously monitor the position of comets and asteroids with near Earth orbits. Optical telescopes with special cameras called charge-coupled devices (CCDs) digitally record millions of images of an area over several minutes. Computer programs scan the images for any change in the orbits of NEOs by analyzing their brightness, direction, and speed. As more data is gathered about a NEO, its orbital path can be predicted more accurately.

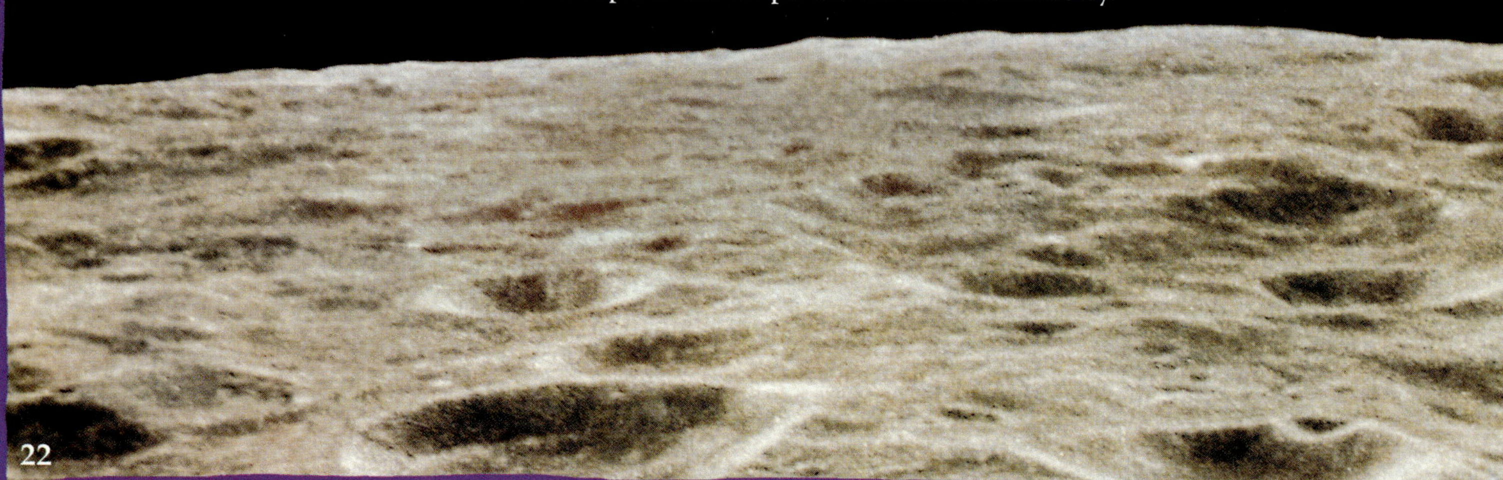

Preventing Earth impact

Before a collision with Earth can be prevented, scientists must consider the NEO's size, speed, composition, and how much time is left before impact. Many space scientists have suggested options for preventing impact. One proposal involves landing a spacecraft on an oncoming asteroid and attaching a rocket to it. If the rocket could generate enough force to move the asteroid when fired, the course of the meteoroid could be altered to avoid collision with Earth. Scientists have also proposed that creating a large explosion with nuclear missiles close to a meteoroid could generate enough force to alter its course. Depending on the size, shape, and composition of the meteoroid, nuclear explosives could also be used to break it up into smaller pieces to pose less of a threat to Earth.

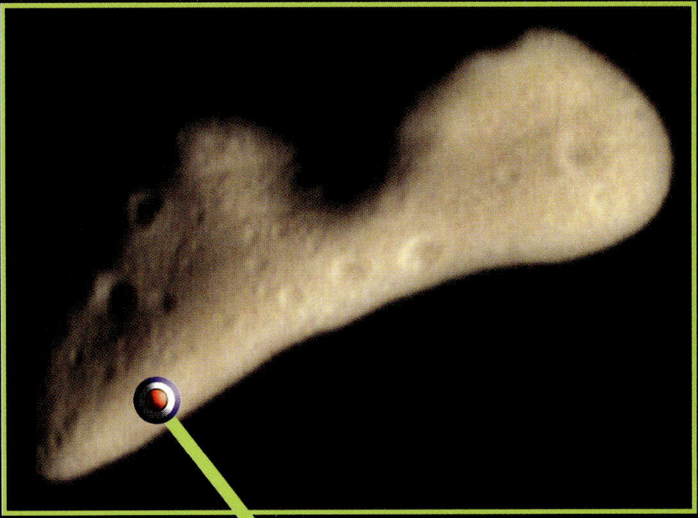

A spacecraft with automated machines in place of a human crew successfully landed on the large asteroid Eros in 2001. The mission proved to scientists that landing a spacecraft designed to divert a meteoroid's collision with Earth is possible.

Safe Space Travel

Space exploration disasters cost millions of dollars and result in the tragic loss of human life. Careful planning, strict safety regulations, pre-mission training, and test flights are some strategies used by space agencies to reduce the risk of disaster.

Preparation

Space agencies must consider every possibility for disaster when planning missions. To ensure the safety of the crew and the success of each launch, every calculation is rechecked, the spacecraft and equipment is inspected, and a backup plan is devised for unpredicted events. **Physicists** and engineers spend years designing, building, and testing equipment to ensure that it will do the job that it is designed for. Astronauts are trained in emergency procedures, and perform simulations under harsh conditions to ensure that they will be able to perform their tasks in space. Even with all of these precautions, accidents still happen. Human error, equipment malfunctions, extraordinary circumstances, and budget restrictions all contribute to space disasters.

(above) Before launching into space, astronauts receive underwater training, which simulates the weightlessness they experience in space. Astronauts practice space walks and space station operations.

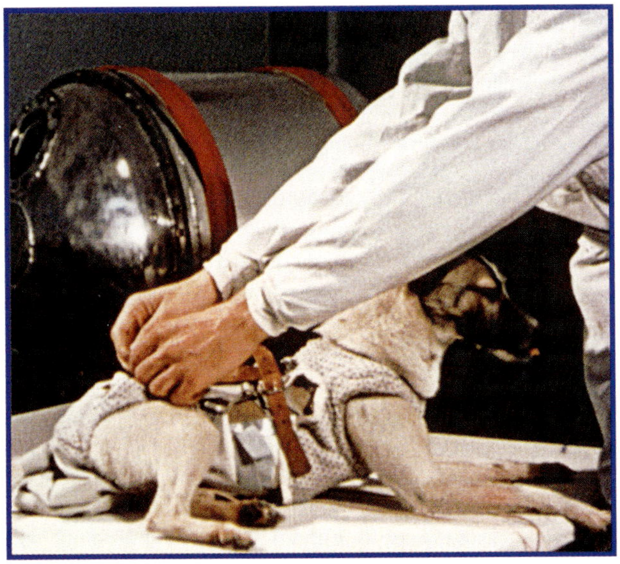

(above) Journalists nicknamed Laika, the first Earthling to achieve Earth orbit, Muttnik. Huskies are called "laika" in Russian.

Animals in space

To learn more about the effects of space travel on humans and to make way for later missions, animal astronauts were used in potentially dangerous missions. During the 1950s, the Soviet Space Agency used dogs for many **sub-orbital flights.** On November 3, 1957, a Siberian husky named Laika was launched into space in the satellite Sputnik 2. Electrodes monitored Laika's breathing, blood pressure, and heartbeat. It is believed that after fours days in space, Laika died when the cabin overheated. Unlike later spacecrafts designed to parachute into the ocean to be recovered, Laika's satellite was not designed to do so. On April 14, 1958, after orbiting the Earth 2,570 times, the satellite lost altitude and burned up in the atmosphere.

Successful Animal Flights

A chimpanzee named Ham was used in a flight aboard the Mercury-Redstone 2 to test his ability to perform tasks under the harsh conditions of takeoff, weightlessness in space, and atmosphere reentry. The rocket was launched at a speed 5,000 mph (8,000 km/h) faster than it should have been, and sent Ham into the upper atmosphere for almost two minutes longer than planned. The error caused the vessel's landing zone to be almost 122 miles (200 km) off course for its predicted landing area in the Atlantic Ocean. After spending nearly three hours bobbing in the ocean, the capsule was recovered and Ham was found to have miraculously survived the flight. This test flight paved the way for the first manned sub-orbital flight by United States astronaut Alan B. Shepherd in May of 1961.

Aftermath of Disaster

A large meteorite impact on Earth would result in major social, ecological, economic, and political changes. Space exploration disasters affect the future of space missions and the progress space exploration has made in understanding science and civilization.

Species extinction

Studies of soil, rock, and sediment layers around impact craters have provided **paleontologists** with evidence that many plant and animal species became extinct following meteorite hits. In the 1970s, geologist Walter Alvarez discovered a layer of clay containing large deposits of iridium, a metal found in meteorites, in rock samples in Italy. The iridium layer dates back 65 million years to the transition from the Cretaceous Period, when dinosaurs roamed the Earth, to the Tertiary Period, when large animals and plants were replaced by smaller species. Alvarez proposed that a meteorite impact caused the extinction of the dinosaurs and other species.

(above) Many geologists believe that a meteorite impact was responsible for the widespread species extinctions that happened 65 million years ago.

Effects of a meteorite collision

The speed of a meteor 6.21 miles (ten km) or more in diameter traveling through Earth's atmosphere causes a huge buildup of energy in the form of heat. Scientists believe this could result in a large explosion or fireball. A meteor of this size could blast a crater eight miles (13 km) deep and as large as 186 miles (300 km) in diameter. Such a collision causes a great amount of dust and rock debris, or ejecta, from the Earth's crust to be thrown up into the atmosphere, and results in what scientists refers to as an impact winter. The ejecta could block the sunlight for months or even years, killing vegetation and the animals that depend on it for food. The debris could also contribute to **global warming**, forest fires, and acid rain, polluting the world's fresh water.

Aftermath of a failed mission

Following an unsuccessful mission, space agencies, the public, scientists, and victims' families look for an explanation for the failure. Critics say costly miscalculations are an example of poor management and planning, and poor use of funds by space agencies. Disasters could also result in a nation's government and taxpaying public to lose interest in funding future missions. When costs are cut on space exploration projects, future missions run a greater risk of failure, since shortcuts may be taken in building and testing equipment, and safety precautions may be sacrificed.

(below) NASA shuttle launches were postponed and canceled after the Challenger disaster. Investigators worked to find the cause of the explosion so that similar accidents could be avoided in the future. The public also needed time to recover from the loss of life and money involved.

The Challenger crew: (front row left to right) Michael Smith, Francis Scobee, Ronald McNair (back row left to right) Ellison Onizuka, Sharon Christa McAuliffe, Gregory Jarvis, and Judith Resnik.

Living Through Disaster

In the event of an unavoidable global catastrophe, the survival of the human race would depend on the advance preparations made for the coming disaster, and the ability to adapt to a changing environment.

Advance preparations

If a meteorite collision with Earth becomes unavoidable, scientists will need to focus on how to live through it. With enough advance warning of a disaster, a portion of the world's population would be able to build underground shelters, stockpile food and fresh water, and evacuate areas most directly affected by the impact. It is unlikely that the world's entire population could escape the immediate effects of the collision. These advance preparations would be limited to those fortunate enough to have access to necessary resources.

Meteorite impacts in Earth's history have had major effects on Earth's life forms. If humans survived a major meteorite impact today, they would need to adapt to the limited food and water supply, and changed climate and environment.

(above) *In 1859, scientist Charles Darwin proposed his theory of natural selection.*

Adapting to a new environment

The Yucatan meteorite wiped out animal species that weighed more than 55 pounds (25 kilograms), which included dinosaurs, about 90 percent of marine animals, and about 85 percent of land animals. The species that survived the impact included small mammals, birds, fish, lizards, crocodiles, and some **invertebrates**. To explain why some species survived, biologists have relied on the theory of natural selection, which suggests that some organisms have characteristics well-suited to an environment that allow them to survive and reproduce. Small species survived because they required little food and water, and were able to adapt to different climates. Larger animals were forced into extinction from starvation, and because they were unable to adjust their body temperature to the changing climate conditions.

(below) An asteroid impact in an ocean can cause a giant tsunami, or tidal wave. The impact would destroy coastal civilizations and ecosystems, flood low-lying inland areas, and wipe out a great percentage of the Earth's population.

Recipe for Disaster

This activity will allow you to recreate the formation of a crater from the impact of a meteorite on Earth.

What you need:

* a baking tray or pizza box lid
* flour to fill the tray
* 1 cup of chocolate cocoa
* a large marble
* string
* tape
* newspaper
* safety goggles

* This activity is messy, so cover the floor with newspaper or create your crater outside.

* Wear safety goggles to protect against flour, or "ejecta" from getting into your eyes.

What to do:

1. Spread the newspaper out on the floor. Fill the baking tray to the top with flour and sprinkle a thin layer of chocolate cocoa over top. Place the tray on the newspaper.

2. Tape the string to the marble.

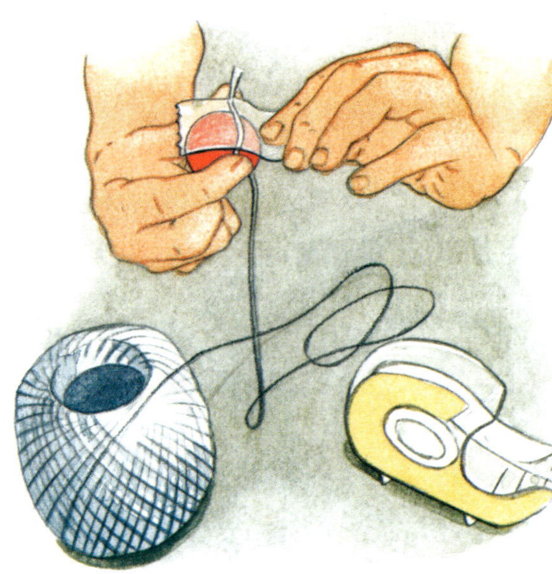

3. Dangle the marble over the tray, then let go.

4. When the flour is settled, use the string to pull the marble out.

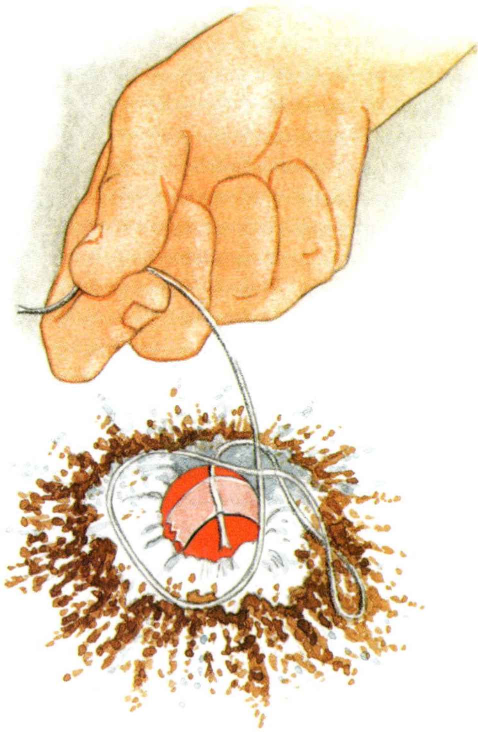

What you will see:

The impact of the marble will cause the flour to spray out from underneath the chocolate cocoa. In a real-life meteorite hit, rays of ejecta, or deep-lying rock, scatter over the surface of the Earth surrounding the crater. Scientists study impact craters by using real and model craters, as well as explosions to simulate craters.

Glossary

atmosphere The layer of gas surrounding the Earth and other planets

bubonic plague A contagious, often fatal epidemic disease

cosmonaut A Russian astronaut

Cretaceous Period A geological period during which the dinosaurs and other life forms became extinct

deflect To cause to turn aside or bend

extinct No longer existing in living or active form

famine A great shortage of food that causes widespread hunger and starvation

flammable Able to catch fire easily

friction The resistance objects face when rubbing against each other

geologist A scientist who studies the structure of the Earth

global warming An increase in the Earth's temperatures caused by pollution

gravity The invisible force that pulls all things toward Earth

invertebrate An animal that has no backbone, such as a worm, clam, or insect

microscopic Something that can only be seen and studied through a microscope

molecule The smallest unit of a substance that can exist by itself

nutrient Something that nourishes, or provides food necessary for good health

oxygen A colorless, odorless gas that humans and animals breathe

paleontologist A scientist who studies fossils to learn about prehistoric animals and plants

physicist A scientist who specializes in matter and energy

reserves An amount of a mineral, fossil fuel, or other resource that exists in a particular location

sediment Small pieces of matter, usually sand or stone, that are deposited by water or wind

solar system The Sun and the nine planets and other celestial bodies that orbit it

solar winds Energetic forces from the Sun's radiation

sub-orbital flight A space flight within the Earth's atmosphere

Index

1 2 3 4 5 6 7 8 9 0 Printed in the U.S.A. 4 3 2 1 0 9 8 7 6 5